Tending Broken Stems

An Anthology of Poetry

Austie M. Baird
-Editor, Cover Artist-

Austie M. Baird is a born and raised Oregonian, holding both History and Education degrees from Eastern Oregon University. Long before becoming a wife and mother, Baird connected with the power of the written word, finding healing properties in both reading and writing. She draws strength from the beauty that surrounds her and the overwhelming love of her family.

A.B.Baird Publishing
Oregon, USA

Printed in the United States of America

First Printing, 2018

ISBN 978-1-949321-00-5
Library of Congress Control Number: 2018907149

Cover Art Image by Austie M. Baird

A.B.Baird Publishing
66548 Highway 203
La Grande OR, 97850
USA

www.abbairdpublishing.com

-*Table of Contents*-

-*Dedications*-

For my mom, my brother and of course,
my dad.
This is only the beginning.
-*Kevin*-

To my aunt Lisa- thank you for showing me how to love the whole
world.
-*CD*-

To M, who spurred me to grow into the writer I have become;
and to my family and friends, my constant support through the
journey.
-*Hooves*-

To my husband Glenn who never gives up on me and to those
who never give up on themselves.
-*Kimmery*-

I dedicate these words to you. The one who helped me find my
smile, grow in my faith, and remember how to love. I owe you so
much. Thank you.
-*Jeremy*-

Thank you to the readers , who have gifted my words with your
support and time. I am thankful to Mrs. Mumtaz, lady who gave
me birth and has been my spine throughout my life and Mr. S. L.
Nayak for being the mentor who changed my perspective towards
the life. I am thankful to A.B.Baird Publishing House for the
opportunity and being thorough professionals from the word go.
-*Azhar*-

I'd like to thank my wife, daughter, parents, and sibling for always loving and supporting me in and through every season life brings.
-*B.E. Sampson*-

For you; my rock, my balance, my sanity. For all the times you told me 'yes' when I told myself 'no'. For being our base; upon which we build dreams and catch stars. I love you.
-*Austie*-

Kevin Vargo

Few roots run deeper than those of Northeast Ohioan-turned-Nashvillian, Kevin Vargo. Providing an authentic, genuine and loving level of empathy and understanding in his writing, Kevin admits, however, that he wasn't always in tune with his path of life. It wasn't until the unexpected passing of his father, coupled with his own strife that life began to strike a chord on a much spiritually deeper level to Kevin. With an ability to put even the darkest and broken most parts of life into beautiful words and to make the beautiful even more stunning, Kevin's writing style and influences are born and raised from the deepest roots of blues and rock 'n' roll. Kevin writes from his truest heart, devoting his purpose to remain authentic while making an impact on others, all with the common goal of wanting nothing more than to ensure his mother lives a comfortable life and that he does all he can to provide support to underprivileged inner city youth.

FROM ME TO YOU

as I write you here,
my dear reader,
with your intuitive ear,
I hope you can hear
my desperate cries
crisscrossed
with a heart,
too big by ten-size.

and my passion,
for you, my dear reader,
burning, yearning
straight from these words
to your beautiful, wandering eyes.

  -Kevin Vargo

3:39am-Head Waves

late at night, late at night,
the mind of a master
speeds wild, and
free,
it can roam,
100 miles an hour
in a no-limit type zone.

late at night, late at night,
ideas, they flow smooth
and the blues
play
loud as can be
drowning out noise
that the daytime never sees.

-Kevin Vargo

LOST IN LUST

tonight,
forget about
your Sunday best.
just turn out the lights
unzip your dress
lay on the bed
and let's make
a little 3am mess.

-Kevin Vargo

THE ONLY GIVEN

through all of our lives,
the only given
is that it all begins
and someday, it all ends.

my dear,
it leaves my bones
shaking in awe
to have a living angel like you
right there beside me
as my own slice of heaven
each day,
through it all.

-Kevin Vargo

A WORLD OF ILITIES

vulnerability
is the accountability
of a heart on fire,
the submission of fear
to find true tranquility;
the possibility
of a broken human bound
to be a beautiful hero
full of humility.

and the acceptability
of any and all;
black or white, at some point, we all fall,
for equality is the only way
to overwhelm with civility.

and, my dear, for vulnerability,
it is the busted in us all,
the deepest, blood-soaked truth
behind the human capability.

-Kevin Vargo

MY DEAR MOTHER

cliche, maybe,
but do you ever stop and think
what a wonderful thing
a strong mother can be?

her words, laden with love,
always calming my head,
for the rest of my life,
I will feel the touch
of my dear mother
and the times she laid me to bed.

my mother, your mother,
the greatest of humankind,
caressing our dreams
and catering to our needs -
by nature, the world's queens.

"attitude and effort,"
my dear mother would always say
at the schoolgate,
a voice forever soaked
in my river of life.

what can I say,
my dear mother,
what truly can I say?

to dedicate a mere poem
to you
is impossible to do.

so much more than these words,
my dear mother,
so much more than life,
you mean to me,
for all that you've given
your children shall return.

-Kevin Vargo

YEARS

dancing and diving,
oh, turning and twisting
they hide
and seek the memories
and with us, they climb
the mountains of life,
carrying the boldest love,
yet simultaneously detonating
destruction
amongst us and our own.

for if we do not learn
to beautifully tango with time,
send our egos to reduction
and our hearts
into production,
we fall off the cliff
and heartbreakingly,
all we do
is merely exist.

-Kevin Vargo

NORTHEAST OH(IO)EROIN

up the road
and all around
narcan -
is the new water
in my hometown.

needed for life
before you end up
on the pavement, face down.

across the street
and right next door
to the fentanyl,
dealer is whore.
in my hometown,
there's good people goin' down
there's young ones,
droppin' to the floor
still asking the needle
for more.

to the victims
come questions;
in Northeast Ohio,
until the drugs die,
and people hear the cry

n o b o d y w i n s.

-Kevin Vargo

DANNA

I sat and I watched two people
with shattered hearts
lock eyes for the first time,
and like two autumn leaves
falling at the same speed,

they tended their broken stems

avoiding loneliness
before a halt at the bottom.

as the swift wind grabbed them
from a place they'd never felt,
they landed together
in the corner
of the softest September grass

lighter

than they ever imagined they could feel.

-Kevin Vargo

A WORK OF ART

next time
you have a nervous first date
or a run-in with someone you hate,
try to look that person in the eye
and instead of
"What?" ask, "Why?"
instead of talking about you,
listen and ask them
about all that they've been through,
because they're a human too,
fighting through life
and mending a wound;

when they know you care
about them and their heart
and the sweet world you share,
a moment in time
becomes a work of art.

-Kevin Vargo

COMMUNICATE

your lack
of communication
often does all
of the talking.

-Kevin Vargo

LIFE JACKETS CALLED FORGIVENESS

because when you judge
without any rhyme
or any reason,
the relationship
starts to sink
without either person
ever taking the time
to realize
they are often
in the same boat.

thank god
for life jackets

called forgiveness.

-Kevin Vargo

BEST DAY OF OUR LIVES

the irony that comes
with a statement so powerful
is one that can only be felt
and truly understood
by those who've felt,
and played the same hand
with the same
otherworldly cards
they've been dealt.

I'll never forget it -
"the best day of my life,"
proclaimed my father, to me,
with a smooth waft of whiskey,
"was the day my dad died."

it was in that chaos, I began to see
there was a reason dad's favorite song
was "Papa Was a Rollin' Stone" -
a childhood boy turned man

far too soon
in a home
a house, anything but a home -
full of temptations,
full of The Temptations.

and the irony comes,
my friends,
in that I can say the same as my papa,
the day he died
was the best day of my life.

my papa, though,
was no rolling stone;
a man with a heart so good,
years, simply misunderstood
masked by pain
and thoughts of self-disdain
it was that day
all that he used to say,
all that he ever did

validated.

a posthumous gift,
he gave to me -
to see my soul far beyond
the right now,
to see my soul
for all that it is
and all that it will be,
far sooner than he, himself,
ever had the same life to see.

Otis & Co. phrased it best,
it was the 14th of June,
that day I'll always remember,
yes I will,
cause that was the day
that my daddy died.

-Kevin Vargo

MAYBE

maybe,
it's not supposed to make sense
to a mind, not so dense.
for years, I've tried
to tie it together
to some line -
but why?

I'm alive,
and I can feel.

I can wake up
on a Christmas morning
with a roof over my head
and my back on a bed,
a grace like no other.

And above all,

I can love.
maybe,
that's all there really is to do.

So, Kevin,
for the first time ever,

I love you too.

-Kevin Vargo

(OUR) KING OF SELF DEMISE

seated in his throne,
magic potion in his blood
drenched down
to every broken, battered
and bruised bone,
oh, that king,
the king of our castle,
even with all his queen
and all his heir's love,
he sat so alone.

and the victim, he played
oh, so well,
for the only way
to tame the dragons
in his living hell
was to unleash the demons;
stronger than God's will.

the true demise came
as those demons,
full of determination
were medication prescribed
and alcohol magnified,
a sad story,
but indeed our king,
had no chance to survive.

-Kevin Vargo

POOR BOY KNOWS BEST

"the money, son,
that's what it's all about,"
said the rich man,
demonizing
comfort -
in his designer suit
and slandering
serenity -
all for the lad(ies)
and his snakeskin boots.

"money is freedom,"
said he, to me,
continuing on,
"you know nothing's free!"

I responded, "well sir, I beg to differ,
so to each, their own…"
but before I could finish
he stopped me and said,
"here, I'll just throw ya bone,
here's a twenty,
and maybe we can talk when you're grown."

well years went by
and I'd heard nothing from the man,
still living my life, though,
according to plan.

but from a boy, I had grown
so I picked up the phone;
that widow of the wicked, she
answered,
and much to her despair,

she explained how, for years,
he'd been dead.
"I just don't get it," she said,
"we had it all,
the cars, the house, the money,
and still, he shot himself
right in the head."

and with one more plead,
she apologized on his behalf
for all those years of greed
and asked me,
"poor boy,
from this pain,
how can I be freed;
how ever could I proceed?"

"comfort and serenity,"
poor friend,
I said,
"and forever you'll have
true wealth
until the end."

-Kevin Vargo

ME TO ME

dear past me,

what a liberation it must be
to finally feel free.

sincerely,

a man who can finally see.

-Kevin Vargo

CD

For poet CD, who has been writing since she could hold a pen, writing is akin to breathing and bleeding. With degrees in both British Literature and Creative Writing, it is no surprise that she is a member of two writers groups in Kansas City or that you can find her posting poetry daily on Instagram as poemsandpeonies. An avid reader, CD is also a collector of books; scouring oily floors at garage sales or inside of the free boxes at estate auctions to discover 100 year old words written on mildewed pages. CD takes her love for literature to the next level by hosting a feminist book club every month. In her downtime, she likes to run marathons all over the world- including a recent trip to run the Great Wall of China. CD is a self-proclaimed lover of cheap wine who loves drawing out the stories of strangers; stating, "by glass two, I will analyze our zodiac compatibility- we'd be friends."

ENERGY

They say energy is neither created or destroyed
but transferred- over and over and over again
ocean tides to rugged rock
swelling. crashing. release.
that look from you
my nails your back. your fist my hair
swelling. crashing. release.
me to you. you to me
over and over and over again-
swelling. crashing. release.

-CD

SUN

I am the sun but she is your moon
and your arms around her night
is my unending torment burning bright-
Set above sky her perfect reflection is white-
But I am scars, hotspots from life spitting flames
reaching to be your light, to warm you untamed
Release her and around me spin!
Release her and hold fire-
The fire that burns beneath my skin!

-CD

THE DIFFERENCE

The difference between me and her- she wasn't
flea market glass or unleveled flour
the record that's fuzzy and skips
not lightening bugs or creaky floors
windows open while it rains
and she wasn't grass stains, or night, or stars.
and she wasn't me. she wasn't me.
but none of this ever made
a difference to you.

-CD

CRUMBS

And I did not know laying there with him
if it was forever or crumbs in life's wrinkly hands
But I knew it was a May afternoon
and May afternoons had freckled his nose
and when he touched me he forgot words
and a bird landed close and hands released slow
and I wanted to say stay, please don't go.
but life has minutes and rent and children with our eyes
and it sets suns and spins. spins. spins madly on
and a life worth living has always felt like an ache
like filling with heavy, filling to brim
and he would turn and I would watch him go
and in the seconds and weeks and months turning slow
we will nod and work and swallow it whole
and the two of us loved. we will always know:
and we will do what they say and tell our heart no.
do what they say and tell our hearts no.

-CD

FIST FULL

I had a fist full of longing, and a fist full of you
and release feels like losing half of my star
and it's rain erasing ink. story never read
and it's leaving my home
and it's heavy. heavy. empty.
and it feels like searching
and it feels like reaching
and it feels like falling
and it feels like breaking
breaking.
    bre e a
           k i
                  n
                      g
                       .

-CD

MASK

Your need to wear that mask for them
was more than your need to love me well
But remember I knew every line of your face -
and loved them. Damn it, I loved them all.

-CD

EYES

His eyes those eyes were searching for me
And I knew those hands were the ones
that had always been reaching
between all of our lives
and dust and bone and breaths
I could not take my soul from his-
I could not take my soul from his!
And we knew it old and deep and over again-
But he'd return to the countries
and back to the trees, back to the places
where he promised to take me
but his hands, those eyes
I can not be free!
because in all of his leaving
he never left me.

-CD

INTENSE

He told me I was too intense.
the heat was intense
the summer I sliced my leg open on barbed wire
digging fence, sock stuck red. job wasn't done
cancer on a body half grown
pulpit men preaching my death is a gift
that no no no see heaven is the goal!
and maybe it was over being hit every day
by a man that did not share my blood
that said it was god's will

that my skin be burned hands
like thanksgiving cutouts
Too intense, maybe so.
For I have yet to meet a man
who can look me in the black of my eye
and not turn away.

-CD

SHARD

What I was six
I fell on top of a broken window
Once I realized no one was coming
I stopped screaming
and pulled the shard from my middle.
This is life for some of us.
This has been life for me.

-CD

CONTROL

control. control. control. control. control.
The stones he placed in my pockets.
And the day he saw the way I looked at the ocean
and warned that swimming I would surely drown-
I   ran   to   the   water.
and when my clothes fell heavy to my ankles
weightless,   weightless
       I
         dove
           in.

-CD

WOMAN

Inside the eyes of every woman-
secrets she had to swallow
for the purest love she'll ever make
men who paid her less
demanding smiles she will fake
wedding bells that rang too soon
children ripped from her womb
demons she chased back to hell
and all the lies she's forced to tell
inside the eyes of every woman-
strength I know far too well.

-CD

RAIN

It rained on us, poured.
And you ran for shelter
but I lifted my face in wonder.
That the sky was like silver meteors
needles dropped from tired fists
cold crystals falling quick-
and that sky was like me
suddenly knowing the gray truth
that I would always be standing alone
suddenly knowing it was time to be drenched
in freedom.

-CD

TORNADO

My grandmother watched tornadoes,
sitting on her front porch.
It took me years but
I have learned you stop
running from lightening
once you realize you are
the storm.

MAJESTY   -CD

I too am salt water and air
and can rage high with uncheck fury
and then rock gently, swelling up and back again
holding power in waves to calm my world around
brimming with cell and origin and wonder
This is why I am drawn back
back again. as the tide was unto its depths
this is why my body within the body of mysterious majesty
feels like everything, feels like nothing
feels like me.

-CD   ## DRESS

Days I should have worn the dress that I saved for you:
that morning reading at the park underneath that tree
summer concert my old friend singing life to me
april sun with my aunt strolling through antiques
and every day I thought of it but passed it by too!
are the days I should have worn the dress
that I saved for you.

-CD

FREE

They said life is in that 2000 year old book
but I could see through the damn pages
no nerve or cell like the tree that shaded me
like in you and him and them and she
those naked birds still wet in nest
and I refuse to forget the rest! !
and many can breathe in brick by hymn
but I need crooked lines and oxygen
and on Sundays I'll cut my calloused feet
on rocky climbs- shame released, pain I'll meet
and no one needs to come for me.
I am alive this is enough to be!
bleeding, bleeding, bleeding free.

-CD

SOFT

I have decided to stand
with my heart in my palms
and when the world refuses to reach
and if feels like a thousands knives
that naked, empty burn-
I will not pull it back into my chest
no. bleeding. holding soft
I will offer. offer. offer.
And I will live a life
that beats outside of its cage.

-CD

SMOKE

The purest love I have ever known does not burn clean-
smoke inhaled so deep that heat escapes from our faces
or raging fires from our tongues.
And when I start to get lost in the thick black
and when I swear I can not inhales again-
he reaches for my face,
and breathes every breath he has into my lungs.
No, our love does not burn clean
Smoke though, that's just proof that it burns.

-CD

GOLD

And I knew
he was the man
that in the middle of my sentence
would kiss me on the nose
and hand me a rock he found
as if it were gold.
and that it would be. for us,
always-
gold.

-CD

K. Waters

Kabrie Waters is twenty-one years young, a coffee shop manager, a big sister, and a dog mom. She found she had a passion for writing sometime around fourth grade, but really started to experiment with poetry around 2016. She was born in a small Idaho town, but has lived in several places across America. Most of her time was spent in Oregon which she found to be a mecca of inspiration and variety. She is also a painter, a musician, and an active traveler.

WHEN YOU LEFT US

Your shirt hung out over the chair.
Ironed, and ready for a day that wouldn't start.
Your newspapers from yesterday morning were still scattered,
halfway read, around the kitchen table.
An unfinished crossword puzzle was laid to rest in the glovebox of
    your car
as it sat like a tombstone in your driveway.
They told me you had left us...
I didn't believe them. I figured it had to be a cruel trick...
because it was all here. Your world was on pause
like a film waiting for the return of its audience.
There were no missing fragments.
No abrupt stop to the sunlight casting shadows through the
    windows.
No moment of silence from the blackbirds.
Just rooms...
unchanged,
abandoned,
and somehow colder without you in them.

-K. Waters

COMMITMENT ISSUES

Growing up, we moved a lot.
Names, faces, friends, and houses...
they all passed like polaroids on a conveyor belt.
Stability began to sound too much like loss
and change dangled like an oxygen mask in a plane crash.
Detachment became a voice in my head, always whispering with
    worry when I got too close.
My mother's defenses ignite when the subject is mentioned,
burning through the conversation till it's nothing but dust
left to rest upon the shelf another day.
I suppose she blames herself for my inability to make commitments
but her guilt is misplaced.
I never wished it to be anything more than what it was.
Several years, heartaches, and seemingly reckless decisions later,
I found myself sprawled across a tile floor, clutching a melting pot
    of pills.
All of them with different names,
colors,
and promises of something better.
None of them were created to treat confusion,
or doubt,
or depression,
or my failure to find a fucking purpose to it all.
Had I known how to commit...
Had permanence not started with the same letter as pain...
I'd have let each pill slide down my throat,
to fill every self-inflicted flesh wound.
I'll likely never stay with one person or grow comfortable in the
    same place
or make a plan I'll carry out without snapping beneath its weight.
My commitment issues will keep me lost and lonely...
but they keep me breathing.

They keep my heart half beating
They keep my lips moving for all the lies I have yet to tell,
and the goodbyes that have yet to torment me.

-K. Waters

SELF EXPECTATION

If I turn the music up loud enough
maybe it will deafen me to the disappointment.
If I drink the wine quick enough
maybe I can make my demons dizzy.
If I scrub every fucking surface in this house
till my fingerprints fall down the drain,
just maybe...
The glare beaming from behind layers of dust
will blind me long enough to make me forget
where I am.
Who I am.
And how different it was all supposed to be.

-K. Waters

I WROTE TODAY

I wrote today, for the first time in a long time.
Whether it's a poem or a suicide note...
I'm not certain.
But even if it's poorly written.
Even if it sounds like "Goodbye".
Even if it is only ever heard by my walls...
It gives me something to edit tomorrow.
It gives me something to wake up for.

-K. Waters

MARKS

Days like this
I'm just another poem in a world that's lost its taste for poetry.
Days like this
I'm the leaf that fell into freshly poured cement.
Days like this
Though I know I've made my mark on the world,
I wonder if it was worth the marks
the world has made on me.

-K. Waters

IT'S A MESS

We don't talk about your AA meetings.
Nor do we talk about the atrocities that live in my head.
Because you are addicted to the numbness
and I am addicted to the pain
and somewhere in the middle,
we collide like lost comets.
I help you feel a little more,
you help me feel a little less
and we're a mess...
but somewhere in the clutter is all the pieces
of every nightmare that brought us here.
Every stab wound that shaped our lives.
We're a mess...
but somewhere from the rubble
a castle can be built,
and perhaps from those towers,
we can find a way to heal.

-K. Waters

BROKEN INVENTION

I know your fears grew from the same lonely place as mine.
The tattoo on your arm is the only permanence you've known.
But while we're both waiting for the bomb to drop,
dance with me through the air raid.
Remember how the sirens made us sway
and when it all comes crashing down around us,
know that years from now...
a smile will tip-toe across my lips
when my ears start humming the phantom notes
to the song of our own broken invention.

-K. Waters

THE CREATION OF

Why, when I call you beautiful,
does it sound more like an apology than a compliment?
My Dear, I know all too well of the chaos
that goes into the creation of creatures like you.
The horrors that made you...
they made me too.

-K. Waters

LESSONS IN LOVE

You were worn and weathered when I found you.
I rebuilt your brittle bones with borrowed marrow.
I lent you air leaked from my own lungs.
You said you hadn't felt so young in years but caught up in your
    rejuvenation,
you failed to realize that the drops of youth I carried to your
    fountain
were drained from my own.
The years I peeled from your heart had to be held somewhere for
    safe storage
 and my rib cage had a vacancy.
I am learning that this is what it means to love...
giving someone wings, even if you must clip the feathers from
    your own.
Teaching someone to fly, even if it means they might leave you.

-K. Waters

POSTCARD

Write me a postcard,
from that place you go to when we are lying in bed
and you are staring at the ceiling as if it were made of glass
and the stars were waltzing across the sky for only you.
Write me a postcard,
From wherever you may be when we are speaking
but you are listening to melodies being sung by sirens
that speak in a language only you know.

Write me a postcard,
From that shore you sail to when my hand is holding yours
but your fingers are slipping themselves through piles of fine white
sand.

Write me a postcard,
Tell me you don't want me with you wherever you are.
Write me a postcard,
From the place that is far more beautiful than what I was able to
give you.

-K. Waters

MUSCLE MEMORY

Defeating your demons is the first step.
Second, understand that it's not us they will hurt now,
but those who choose to love us.
Because like a corpse soaks into the soil
They become a part of who we are.
Unseen, but like a phantom limb,
always a part of our muscle memory.
Always the root of our instincts.
Reminding us of our need to survive,
even in the safest of places.

-K. Waters

A STRANGE ALCHEMY

"I Love you more" he said,
and he's probably right.
Love is a chemical in the brain that my body
refuses to produce with the same negligence it once did.
But even with my faulty wiring,
I will continue to love you in whatever artificial way I am able.
With my best efforts
and a strange alchemy,
I am yours.

-K. Waters

MISTAKEN

I have confused the sound of your car engine with my own heart
   beat.
 When you pull up my rib cage starts to rattle from the violent
     pounding and every time you pull away there is an unsettling
     stillness in my chest.
This leaves me wondering if maybe my pulse has become reliant on
     you to pump my blood.
 I try not to think of what would happen to my breathing should
     the crackling of your tires on the gravel ever stop.

I have confused the sound of your voice for my favorite song.
When you speak my body begins to dance without me as if on a
     cue I don't remember being given, as though maybe I was a
     sleeper agent in a past life and my soul was trained to move
     only for yours.
But I wonder if I could remember the steps if you were to stop
     playing.

I have confused you for a home.
Your arms are a door I feel I can walk into without having to knock
    and though I don't take that for granted I should know by now
    that people are not building materials...
They do not make stable shelters.

-K. Waters

SOMEDAY

Someday the fireflies
will learn to live in glass jars.

Someday the flowers
will sprout from rusted kitchen sinks.

Someday shoes
will walk down cobblestone streets,
with no one to guide them.

On that day...

I will unpack my suitcase
and stay still, happily,
in one place.

-K. Waters

MY WORLD

My world is made up of canary colored walls,
rust stains, and hazelnut coffee.
It entangles you with fishnet thighs
and lullabies of the broken people.
My world is a crooked music box ballerina,
a flooded basement floor,
and a jade plant in the windowsill that refuse to grow.
My world is not made up of shining city lights,
chandeliers, or chariots ready to whisk you away.
My world is not a fairy tale, or even a poet's melancholic
    wonderland...
it is ordinary, and messy, and brutal at times.
But I believe with you in it,
our world could be an enchantment among the numbered streets.
I believe with you in it, this world could feel like home.

-K. Waters

INSOMNIAC

I sip coffee stronger than I am with the man on the moon.
we whisper secrets and laugh at the stars listening in,
like the old woman from the corner shop.
I pour my irregular heart beats out to the milky way.
She spins them all in circles until they remember their rhythm.
I sometimes start to believe that my words have run dry...
and then the constellations remind me of all the creation
I am capable of.

-K. Waters

THE GARDENER

Growing up, we didn't have much...
What we did have was our mother,
who was often tired and frail
and looked as though she might cave in at any moment...
but she never did.
She had more fight in her little finger
than most people have in their entire bodies.
She had a way of turning every broken home into a palace.
So we bought a small house on fourth street.
The yard was barren.
the paint was chipped.
the floors and corners were soaked with mold.
The world looked bleak,
but she scrubbed till her fingers bled.
She painted till her arms trembled.
She planted flowers in every ugly corner...
and she taught us that even in hell,
a home can grow.

-K. Waters

PEOPLE LIKE US

Maybe it's people like us,
who never imagined
they might be made of anything more than bones and dust.
Those who know how hopeless the world can appear.
Maybe it's people like us,
that were always destined to hang the stars.

-K. Waters

YELLOW SUNDRESS

I wore a yellow sundress,
hoping to catch the attention of someone kind...
but you found me instead.
You, with your house on the hill,
your soundproof windows,
and your paintings that only depict pain.
You who built your four post bed
knowing full well that it's steel limbs
would be strong enough to break my spirits.

I wore a yellow sundress.
You peeled it away from me,
and then my skin,
and then my sanity.
You with a touch that was only gentle
because it knew there would be no fight.
You who handcrafted my nightmares.
You, who I see in every stranger on the street.
You, whose fingerprints have stained my skin.
You, who turned my body into a crime scene
and made me believe that never again could it be my temple.

You...
whose name I kept from my mother.
You, the father of three...
How can you check for monsters beneath their beds
While you linger below mine with fangs bared and claws
sharpened?

I wore a yellow sundress…
and for the first time in years,
it's threads didn't feel like your hands.
For the first time since then,
I worked up the courage to tell my mother.
For the first time I don't speak of it as though I'm apologizing.
For the first time…

I wore my yellow sundress,
hoping to catch the attention of someone kind.
And this time…
I know the difference.

-K. Waters

-Hooves-

Joseph Interligi, affectionately known as -Hooves- , is a 27 year old writer from Arkansas, USA. He fell in love with poetry at a very young age, as his mother chose to read poetry over fairytales before bed. By the time he had turn eight he was already filling notebooks with his own writing, a habit that he enjoys continuing today. His love for writing is only topped by his love for the environment and adventure. As an avid motorcycle rider he has traveled extensively through the western part of America on his way to fight forest fires in Oregon. He currently is still pursuing his love for the environment as he works for the Arkansas State Parks system.

<u>6/26/17 10:54</u>

I have nowhere to be.
Won't you grant me this one
Request:

Take me with you on your
Leap?

I know I have never shown up
When it was right, but
I'm short on money,
Low on time, and
Just too tired to sleep.

I'm not wanting magic,
Just need something to
Believe.

-Hooves-

<u>6/6/17 6:36</u>

I want to be caught
In your drunken stars,
Stitched into those
Loosely drawn dreams.

I want to be the daring
Wild flower you pick
For the front pocket
On your jeans, folded
Into the colors
Of your memories.

I want to be the sweet
Melody you capture
From the breeze, written
Into the songs with lyrics you loved repeating.

-Hooves-

<u>8/12/17 3:30</u>

The moon was shallow and the sun was gold.
We decided this night was too young to just go back home.
So, I grabbed your hand and felt the wild.

We chased the silver in the dawn
with the sun being the only objector.

-Hooves-

A DANCER IN THE FLAMES

She danced like her world was on fire,
throwing her amber hair with the wind.

You couldn't catch her with your hands,
you had no chance of leading, she twirled too fast for that.

You'd only see her in glimpses
as you chased the tapping of her flats.

You were hers before you knew you were in engulfed,
ready to burn.

-Hooves-

11/27/17 8:58

The closest I've been to perfection
is when you let me steal a kiss.

It tasted like peace,
but the violence was silent.

-Hooves-

2/11/17 5:55

You were so clever.
The way you moved
Those sweet lips...

How easily
I fell for
Those luscious tricks.

You took my hand,
Confidence,
And strength
In your grip.

I gave into everything
My mother told me to beware.

But I guess that's
Why they say love isn't fair.

-Hooves-

7/15/17 3:36

I hoped if I kept persuading the air
To extinguish the flames,
I could secretly claim it as a wish.

If not, I've got fish bones
In my right pocket
&
A rabbit's foot dangled
From my wrist.

I'm not too superstitious,
But I'll take any type of charm
These tokens will give.

The familiar steps have come to a head.
With issues of the heart,
I've stepped into wilderness.

So with fingers crossed,
I hope we share the moon tonight.
It's the only time I feel our hearts
Are on the same side.

-Hooves-

<u>1/26/17 9:56</u>

I hummed something soft and sweet.

I begged her
Never to stop dancing,
Even for me.

I fell wild just for her dreams.

Lips like venom,
The only one who stopped moving
Was me.

-Hooves-

6/3/18 6:33

I still think about you all of the time.

I've considered the fact
I may be broken.

Maybe I'm a record,
with that perfect skip,
where I replay the same verse
until I'm sick.

That's it:
I must be sick,
They say time is the cure to all
but your name is still tattooed
on my lips.

Every hello, every kiss,
every night of sinful bliss
I wake up to the fact
that none of it tasted
like those moments I miss.

I know, I need to get a grip.
Trust me, It's crossed my mind
more than I'd like to admit.

But here I am still spilling words,
thinking maybe one more sentence
will rekindle a spark I snuffed out,
not knowing it would be my only wish.

-Hooves-

1/14/18 7:44

It's taken all my life to find halos around street lights
that have no need for the horizon,

As if they spark with coils, suffocating mistakes,
attempting to mimic snakes.

So, I ask, how can someone forget when they've chosen as a living
to wade in a sea of memories, like islands in search of the shores
that decided to retreat.

-Hooves-

7/16/17 6:25

You broke me into a million pieces
That did not float but
Plummeted to the ground.

These pieces were trampled and kicked
All across your foot prints.

I meant to mend myself back together
As the jigsaw I would need to become,
But with the pieces still stuck
To your soul, I created a mosaic,

Becoming a sight to behold.

-Hooves-

<u>11/14/17 8:47</u>

Today, I found another fault,
Shaking what was unknowingly built within its reach.
Foundations draped in belief
considering the stones were laid by hand.

Building on pillars bolted to sediments of trust,

I found another fault today;
I'm rebuilding.

-Hooves-   <u>5/7/18</u>

I woke up this morning from dreaming about my darling,
so I laid back down.

I try to sleep as much as I can, ever since the view became baked
dust and mountains of sand.

I couldn't imagine this room becoming much bleaker.
Well, I also never imagined she could leave.

I'm doing better now though.
My heart doesn't flood over the steps when I hear the stoop creak.

I've become comfortable with this new type of free,
this new type of identity,

This new type of film that defines what I've been missing.

Loving.

-Hooves-

4/27/18

I've been living a life that would make Sisyphus wince.

Chewing on boulders, making a mess out of hardy teeth.

I've been caught in the rain, the undertow, the westerly winds.

But still here I am.

I've been burned to a crisp, left without a wish, dreaming about how things could have been.

But still here I am.

I've smiled in front of pain, laughed in front of grief, walked away from death as she snarled her teeth.

But still here I am.

So what is next they always ask, when I've lived a life many would choose to pass.

I chuckle and say,
"Can't you see? I'm still here and for that I'm counting blessings."

-Hooves-

8/5/15: BETTER MIDDLE MAN

Everything I could never say
I confide in the stars.
Hoping the moon is a better
Middle man
Than my heart.

-Hooves-

10/23/15: ARKANSAS TRAVELER

My love
Settled in
Another
Plot.

It became
Too hard to
Bloom

In
Your
Garden.

-Hooves-

<u>4/12/17 4:23</u>
She dances in the rain,
Not to wash away
The ashes of her past,
But to believe
Magic can still
Fall freely.

She leaps from
Puddle to puddle,
Crashing into little seas,
Giving a second chance
For unfulfilled wishes
To fall again.

-Hooves-

<u>3/26/17 9:43</u>

She never wondered
What he would do with her heart.

Would it be a mantel piece? Art?

She never questioned
If it would be splintered or torn apart.

She only lit his way through the dark.

-Hooves-

5/25/16 6:33

Her kiss was a delicate drop
Sitting on his lips as dew
Every morning,

Revitalizing his petals
That were beat by the
Summer glare.

She became so instrumental
To his growth and recovery,
He began to wish away his hours
Till the sun turned over.

The dawn was his idea of home,
Where her kiss lingered for,
What seemed to be,
Forever.

His kiss was the force
That pushed hard on her heart
As the sun set each night.

The slivered moon revitalizing her soul
With a glimmering light.

The dawn, the night,
They twist,
They fight.

For the same thing, forever.

-Hooves-

<u>3/11/18</u>

As I am surrounded by only drumming rain, twisting wind, and trembling thunder, she raised from a slumber with a smile of sunshine I knew I'd been missing.

With sails frayed to the seams and barley clinging to the mast; I knew then, this battered ship would make it home. She became my harbor. My port.

-Hooves-

A SUMMER BEE

I've been wasting my life trying to make sense of the fact that I shouldn't have ever taken flight.
How can these little wings, battered and bruised, keep carrying me to something new?

Landing on flowers, looking for urgency, risking that my baggage might be heavier than what the stem was expecting...

But it does not break; it holds me stout, just like these wings that carried me from a place of doubt.

-Hooves-

Kimmery Moss

Kimmery Moss was born and raised in Southern California. She was educated at the University of Southern California, graduating with a degree in Creative Writing and a minor in Political Science. She taught middle school English for several years and is now dedicated full-time to writing. She enjoys living in the Inland Empire with her husband, two dogs, and four chickens.

SUMMER STORMS

I'd be the rain, the warm summer rain
dropping in on you
in the middle of a pleasant lunch, or
perhaps a brunch

I drip
      drip
            drip
                  into your drink
inviting you to look up at me, with difficulty.

I baptize you with warm water
      one in your eye, you blink
            the hell is this? you think
Some dance in me, bare skinned
      as I quench desert lands,
            pooling in their sands
Sawing palms with my breeze
whipping up Caribbean seas
rocking boats, flooding moats
I thunder—
      while you all run under roofs
      awnings, trees
disappearing fast, drying quickly
leaving some feeling free
leaving only a memory.

-Kimmery Moss

PAIN

It came in, uninvited
strutting, tail wagging
mine, between my legs

it stopped when it saw me
a slow smile spreading
and gave me something I did not
want
but needed.

I tried to give it back, but—
No,
No, you don't get to trade pain
like that.

-Kimmery Moss

ORIGAMI

He folds himself
delicately
into origami—
a new shape every time

unfolding

reshaping

ignoring old creases.

He folds himself into a crane
a paper airplane—
anything
anything
anything to avoid his pain.

-Kimmery Moss

ANOTHER MOON

another moon,
another month,
another mixing
of us.

How silly I was,
thinking we won't change
when all this time it was—
the rose budding,
the leaves falling,
the fires
roaring,
the forests
burning
then alive again
after their deaths
trying to teach me
that everyday the earth will
change
and so will I.

-Kimmery Moss

ARRANGMENTS

and so, this is how it goes
she thought
as she bent
to collect the pieces
of herself
and
arranged them into a bouquet
to share them
with another.

-Kimmery Moss

MIRROR WORK

This is what I want:
Desirability
A—a—a—lack of shame
The load I lug,
shrugged.

Why is perfect so sexy?

It lures me in

It strokes my face
It whispers in my ear
A soft and sultry voice—
and I like it
though I know it is a lie.

-Kimmery Moss

APPETITE

How many wants
      equal a life?

Will you run through them quickly
      burn your cash
      throw one back
      run with the pack

or move slow, instead
      every sip of tea tasted
            every sunset savored
                  every love leaned into—

your want in your back pocket
your heart up front?

-Kimmery Moss

SOAK

I soak in hot, hot water
oils and salts
all my past faults.

If I correct them, quickly
will they remember who I was?
I was
I was someone else, then
and another someone tomorrow—

No need to erase.
No need to explain.
The beauty is in the change.

-Kimmery Moss

MITOSIS

A pebble fell
at the center of my forehead
then my body,
fragile
split down the middle.

Each of my organs chose a side to belong to.
      My right half fell onto the sidewalk
      and it spilled and it spilled and I gasped.
      I spilled muscle, I spilled blood while
my left side wobbled but stood upright.
I thought, how odd to be still living with intestine
exposed and only one leg to walk on.

The left of me left—
went for a hop through the park
and I wondered if my horizontal side
was my weaker side as a bird stopped by to sing
awhile and perch on the shoulder I still had.
I thought of abandonment, of and by my selves
while a tree above me dropped a tiny spring blossom
which glued itself onto my liver
still moist from the split.
The sun warmed me, burnt me,
caused a sweet stench to rise.

Which half of me would they write about in the books,
which half of me still had a heart?

-Kimmery Moss

IT COMES

It comes.

It comes
        like waves
  the joy
        and the sadness too.

Ride them.

Ride them
        closer to shore
each time.

-Kimmery Moss

CONVERSATIONS WITH GOD

When breath is short
and you
you
you don't see a way—

Remember:
Mountains move too.

They just take their time.

-Kimmery Moss

BIOLUMINESCENCE

The swaying creaky mast
from where I see it, far below,
looks as if it sweeps across the sky,
windshield-wiping stars from my eyes.

Our hull bounces across the salty waters,
jolting us from one side to another.

The darkness is heavy here
and we grab onto the railings,
                    onto the lifelines,
                              onto each other

The stars never budge, though,
except the ones we find in the ocean:
some lighted little creatures
that awaken in our wake—
the fireflies of the sea
slipping past us
as we trudge forth
in our ocean passage.

I feel lucky as I begin to realize
that everything is illuminated
and has been all along.

-Kimmery Moss

INFINITE

My shovel hits ground,
                again.
Only it has changed, the ground—

Impossibly solid when I first dug
then muddy, after storms
then loose and falling to pieces
when I hit it last.

I dig,
        I dig,
                I dig deeper still
and like an ocean
I do not end.

-Kimmery Moss

SEQUOIA STAMINA

I am,
I am, she said
to the trees,
looking down at knobby knees
so free,
and yet rooted down
growing up
seeing the sun through clouds
gaining strength
with every rain.

-Kimmery Moss

THE HUMAN

I touch

I tangle

I toss around
the parts of me
the darkest shades of black
the flowers that bloom from pain
A—a—a puzzle of hues
A hot-blooded fuse

I am
I am
The survivor of me
The one who hurts and heals,
The human.

-Kimmery Moss

SPACE

The inexplicable
Void
Starry skies,
What lies between thighs
A pause, after uttered words
The air between us—
tense or sweet
sweet space
within us
What we take up
and what we leave
when we go.

-Kimmery Moss

HOME

Water on lips,
Hands on hips,

I welcome you.

You, the human
You,   the bringer of light
You,   both healer
and hurter
because you are me
and you are he
and you are she
walking in sand
while waves come to erase
mistakes.

-Kimmery Moss

I RAN

I ran, feverishly
to all parts of everything
to taste it
to drink it in.

I reached for fistfuls of wind
and ether and light
of earth and dust and words—

More, and faster
I drank, I saw, and I felt it all.

And why,
        why,
            why
they asked,
did she make it about everything
when she went to look for
herself?

Oh, but— they did not know
they did not know
that everything is me
and I
I am everything.

-Kimmery Moss

Alice Foster

Alice P. Foster is a 20-year-old writer from the beautiful seaside town of San Diego, California. After discovering the poetry anthology of her late father, Chad Albitre, she fell in love with the written word and the way it can speak to even the deepest parts of one's soul. It is her hope that her words can serve as a gentle reminder to look for the hidden miracles in life that are all around us; whether they appear in nature, the kind word of a friend, or even a tragedy that was simply a blessing in disguise.

AND AT THAT MOMENT

and in that moment
all of the color
drained from the world's face
when everything was perfect
and nothing hurt.

i am being drowned
in this ocean
that is replacing my skin:
i am the water that won't let you
sink through.

if you look at the sky
over los angeles
at 5am
you will see a color
that didn't exist before.

it will hold you in its mouth
like a new mother.
like all of the questions
we place in god's hands.

-Alice Foster

SOFT WHISPERS

soft whispers
replacing marrow

sleepless in the middle of a dream

this love
swallows its victims
whole.

-Alice Foster

A DARK STRAND

a dark strand of hair
coils around my ankle
in the bath.
the water is a muted green now
and the numbing warmth
is beginning to wear off.
i am beginning to hear
sound again.
my eyes open
to the fluorescent light fixture
above
and almost mistake it
for your face: the way it looms over me
like a guardian angel,
an unholy sun.

healing is not always beautiful.
sometimes it is making eye contact
with the driver next to you
after crying for hours
in your car.
sometimes
it's walking to the other side
of the room
for a second glass of water.
sometimes it's apologizing
to your birds
for never having the energy
to clean their cage
or standing up in the bath,
drying yourself off
with a clean towel,
and brushing the tangles
from your matted hair.

-Alice Foster

THIS BODY

this body is a wound
that will continue to heal.

-Alice Foster

LISTEN TO THE AIR

listen to the rising air
escaping your lungs:

how the body collapses
and rebuilds itself
with every leaving breath.

-Alice Foster

TURN THE COLORS

turn the colors
your bruises have given you
into sunsets
and let every painting be a reminder
of how fearless life has made her child.

-Alice Foster

THE PROCESS

the process of growing wings
is painful
but remember,
one day they will lift you
far away from here

-Alice Foster

PRECIOUS GENTLE THING

precious, gentle thing
one day you will remember
what you truly are.

there is no beginning
and there is no end
to you and me.

we are all made of stardust
and a love
more blinding than the sun.

-Alice Foster

GRACE FOUND ME

grace found me
by the water
one spring day:

jacaranda petals
cradled in a river
of velvet light

the crane
lifting her ancient wings
to greet the morning sun

and the thought of you
like a gentle word from god

floating effortlessly
downstream.

-Alice Foster

SUNLIGHT REFLECTED

sunlight reflected
in pale irises
resembles nothing short of god.

i saw him in my room last night.
i thought it might have been you
standing by the door.

once you have seen the light
darkness no longer seems
so comfortable.
i stayed awake for days
imagining what it would look like.

if you pray long enough
eventually someone will hear you.

i know this
because you're here.

-Alice Foster

YOU ARE THE ONE

you are the one
i look for in crowded rooms.

you are the light
swallowing this tunnel
Whole.

-Alice Foster

THE SOUND OF THE CHRASHING WAVES

the sound of crashing waves
is braided
with the rhythm in your chest.

what happened to you?
how did the ocean fit itself
inside your body?

-Alice Foster

HEAVEN

heaven
is not hiding on the other side
of towering golden gates
but a gaze warm enough
to thaw life's touch.

-Alice Foster

YOU AND I

you and i have cosmic blood
running through our veins.

we are from the same
crease in god's hand:
the same unfolding star

-Alice Foster

IN A SEA

in a sea
blooming with stars
i would still find the one you came from
and hold it close to my skin
because it has always belonged to me.
even before my name was ever spoken
yours was sewn into the walls
of my mother's womb
and the angels who sing me to sleep every night
laugh with each other
because they have seen it:
every perfect moment
and every sky
waiting to open before our eyes
when the future is finally close enough
to touch.

i have seen life
as a child
who sits quietly
and smiles
even with no one around.

-Alice Foster

IT'S IN THE WAY HE LIFTS ME

it's in the way he lifts me
so effortlessly,
as if i didn't carry entire lifetimes
beneath my skin.
it's the way i've forgotten them.
it's the warmth that kisses me
to sleep every night
and the fear that leaves
before i can catch up to it.

it's the way we breathe
without hesitation:
how our lungs have stopped fighting
how our hands open towards the light.

heaven
is a place found
only in the distance
between irises.

Alice Foster

J.B.

Hailing from a small southern town in Georgia and becoming a world traveler as an active duty Army Major, author Jeremy Brown writes collections of thoughts and feelings based on his life experiences. Be it the physical description of being with a woman, the emotional portrayal of a broken heart, or the thrill of being alive; he writes with raw emotion that echoes through one's soul. In his own words, "The ink is my blood and I leave a small part of myself for her in every piece of my prose."

STAY OR GO

Would you have stayed,
if I'd have pushed the issue?

If I shared with you,
the horrors that keep me awake at night?

If I showed you,
the blood that flows through my body to prove I'm human?

If I fucked you harder,
instead of being gentle?

If I bared my soul,
and the secrets that live within?

If I pulled your hair,
while appreciating your back?

Or would it all be for naught,
and the answer would still be me watching you
walk away?

-J.B.

BIGGEST LIE

Perhaps the biggest lie you've ever told
is the one where you told me you're not the one
and we're better off without one another.

-J.B.

NOT ENOUGH

I hope you never experience the pain of being told
100% of your love and effort
isn't enough.

STILL YOURS

-J.B.

I wasn't perfect
but I was yours and,
the fucked up thing about it is,
I still am.

So, when you finally get your heart broken
by "The One",
just come home and wake me from this coma called life.

-J.B.

NOT READY

As bad as I want the nightmares to stop,
I'm not ready to let go of the memories of us.

-J.B.

BROKEN PIECES

I leave a trail of my broken pieces
hoping maybe one day she'll collect them,
find her way back
and make me whole again.

-J.B.

I WONDER

I wonder
if she looks at the pictures of my smile
as often as I revisit the ones of hers.

-J.B.

SECURITY

I miss laying my head in your lap,
your fingers running through my hair
and the feeling of security I've never had before.
That as long as my head was there,
in your hands,
nothing could hurt me.

-J.B.

I WILL NEVER...

I will never apologize with, "I love you."

The three most meaningful, yet overused, words in the English language,
and I still remember when I said them to you,
but more importantly,
I remember where my heart was at the time.

-J.B.

THESE WORDS

We may not be,
but you'll always have
the most important pieces of me.

My words are the most valuable things I own,
and you have them all
in place of the love I haven't shown.

-J.B.

NOT MINE

I'm not good at keeping things that no longer belong to me.

Once we've had a romantic relationship,
please don't pressure me to be friends.
It's not that I no longer care,
it's just that I'll always love you
and I can't handle the pain of seeing someone else
provide you with what I couldn't.

-J.B.

THE BURDEN

My only wish is for your happiness.
With me or without me.
I have no problem carrying the burden of a broken heart
 for you to find the love you want.

-J.B.

TEACHERS

Sometimes those who teach us the most throughout our lives
are there for the shortest periods of time.

-J.B.

MY CROSS

I struggle to bear
the weight of the memories
from when we were happy.

Oftentimes those thoughts seek to bring me to my knees,
but what allows me to sleep
is knowing we are both better versions of ourselves
for having spent time
in one another's lives.

-J.B.

INTOXICATING LOVE

In the end,
the intoxicating love they shared
was worth the pain and failure it resulted in.

-J.B

POWERFUL MEDICINE

Seeing photos
of someone you used to love
without feeling the knife reenter your heart
is powerful medicine.

-J.B.

HER MISSION

She's been on a mission for as long as she can remember.

Not to find herself,
for she knows exactly who she is.

Not to find a destination,
for she knows exactly where she is, is where she needs
to be.

Her mission is to find a man worthy enough to match her stride
through the unexplored
without strangling her thirst for the unknown.

-J.B.

MULTIDIMENSIONAL

You're multidimensional.
You have so many layers of kindness, warmth, sensibility,
messiness, love and compassion
that I'm left trying to figure out what group of angels made you
and weren't smart enough to keep you for themselves.

-J.B.

THE REAL THING

I stood by
as my father watched the love of his life
pass before his eyes.

He watched
her wither away
for over two years as she fought cancer;
a huge "fuck You" smile on her face the entire time.

The love and desire in his eyes was unwavering
and uncompromising
throughout.

That's the kind of love I convey
when I say
"I love you."

-J.B.

ACROSTIC LOVE

Honestly, I had my doubts that
Our relationship would
Last, but I'm in your debt for
Loving me even when
You knew from the start I
Just didn't love myself,
And together we stood with the
Grace and compassion in our hearts.

-J.B.

WITH YOU

When I'm with you I have no insecurities.
When I'm with you I'm completely comfortable.
When I'm with you I feel no anxiousness.
When I'm with you I let down my defenses.
When I'm with you I can smile.
You tear down my walls,
fill my heart and make me feel complete.

-J.B.

ONLY HOPE

I can only hope that, in the distant future,
someone will find one of my writing notebooks
and have no doubt the amount of love
I have for you.

-J.B.

CUDDLING

He never wanted to cuddle for long because he gets hot however,
when he felt her soft rhythmic breath on his chest,
her leg resting inside his,
their hearts beating in synch,
the pressure of her breasts against his ribs and her thick,
sweet smelling hair gliding through his fingers
he knew two things.
She was finally at peace with the world
and it would never be too hot to have her body on his.

-J.B.

I'LL BE THERE

When your body isn't as tight
and when your mind begins to fade,
I'll be there.

When you can't get up the stairs
or remember my name,
I'll be there.

Just as surely
as the same stars come out every night
as the first night my lips touched yours,
I'll be there.

-J.B.

Born Maverick

Azhar Murtuza is a Biotech engineer with master's degree in International Business from Queen's University, Belfast. He is an active Rotarian and Human Rights activist besides being an entrepreneur himself. Being an avid traveler and empath has helped him transform his various life experiences into written words. His willingness to travel less taken paths in his daily life has gifted him his identity and hence the ink name- Born Maverick.

HOLD ON

Let me take you away
To the place where you belong
With my words being the guide
And your presence to glide
I promise to take you on a journey
Where the world is less of a truth
And the love is more of a reality
Just hold on for some time
Let's make a moment
For a lifetime.

-Born Maverick

CONFESSIONS

You saw my heart burning
My eyes raining
And my skin breaking apart
But all you didn't see
Was my virgin soul
Which was never touched for once
As the hands which felt me
Ran through my breath
Like a shot of whiskey
On a cold night of winter
But never settled for it.
As they always knew
There was a summer
Just around the corner.

-Born Maverick

MYSTIC CHARM

I spilled every emotion
In a cold river of certitude
But not a drop melted
Under the warmth of compassion
As my own words dried up
Blocking a channel of estuary
And now I seal every letter
In between my lips
As I swallow all syllables
Every time my heart
Tries to articulate love
On platform of conveyance
As I rain dance in tears
Which were once a cloud
Formed by your
Mystic charm.

-Born Maverick

FADING IN DARKNESS

Streaming into my dreams
You turned out to be a reality
A virtue of fervour to be held upon
I tried opening my eyes to you
As every blink of an eye
Stopped the beat of my heart
Only to breathe in your existence

And just when I found my sunshine
I saw you fading in darkness.

-Born Maverick

ZONE OF DESTINY

I was short of words
And I found poetry in you
I was lacking for thoughts
When I found a pretty muse in you
My life was low on hues
When I found an art in you
As at every step of my life
I was finding a way in you.

But being lost in the zone of destiny
All that I could not find
Was a home in you

-Born Maverick

AN INCOMPLETE STORY

Your pin drop of silence
Turned out to be a brick in my life
Elevating as an invisible wall
While all I advocated was a rescue
By searching for a broken silence
As I waited for your words
Being stuck at the same page of life
Which you left half written
Only to destine me
As an incomplete story.

-Born Maverick

REVEALING EYES

We walked several miles
Holding the hands of love
Under the shades of destiny.
But never we knew that
Even a single step in future
Would be a struggle
On our own.

I see our smiles of past
Dripping through our eyes
At present.

-Born Maverick

ALWAYS GREY

Happiness was to swim across
But I found solace in drowning
Life was all about moving on
But I savored the pain of clinging.

For me,
Love wasn't all about
Trying to win
But it's all about losing yourself.
Not white
Not black
But it's always grey.
An inseparable phase
Which is here to stay.

-Born Maverick

GUARDED DESTINY

I could dance away
A million stars
Yet my heartbeat
Was locked in a moon
As it always remained
A touch away
And a word away
While she made sure
To take my breath away....

Few wishes remain a stretch away
With a guarded destiny.

-Born Maverick

A BATTLE OF THOUGHTS

I took your words
Placed them in my heart
Caged it with feelings
And dressed it with love
But all I failed
Was to lock my mind
Which knew it was all a game
And here I stand
Fighting a battle of thoughts
Which can never be won
As my heart and mind
Refrain to agree as one.

-Born Maverick

ASH OF FERN

Those fiery flames induced on my bruised heart
Are the token of your calmative depart.
Craving to kindle and forming into ashes
Is my last resort.

Enslaved to your edict, I await for my turn
Succumbing to your warmth was my only yearn.
Split to solitude,
I replicate an ash of fern.
Given my musings is now all said and done,
Now I fancy smolder and won't return
As no ocean seems colossal to heal my burn.

-Born Maverick

FADED MEMORY

Few steps from me, I see you standing.
I feel to hug you,
But actuality keeps me stranding.
I am the same,
You are the same
Priorities have become devils own game
And knots of togetherness are now just tame
As we have burnt to ashes in this love flame.
But trust me,

Only thing etched on my heart
Is your name.
Pretty girl is now a lady of social matter
Chivalrous boy is a man now taking life's batter.
Once a pair blended with perfect imperfections
Have been broken due to imperfect perfections.

Same world but different territory
Two bodies, one soul and same old story
As we are only left with
Faded Memory.

-Born Maverick

EVANESCENCE

I await an arduous night ahead
Reminiscence of you is making me dread
Incarnation of intimacy is a dream now dead
And your love is just a canvas in haunted museum.

My night has just begun,
And my eyes already numb.
Your mojo scent is still running in my breath
Which was once,
A fragrance of my life
Is now tugging me to pernicious death.

Indeed, you touched my soul
Only to gift venomous scars all over
But I wasn't the one to roll over
As I wish I could wile you for once
Just before it all becomes,
Evanescence.

-Born Maverick

CHIEF

Every time a step climbed
He fell a mountain down
Yet, personified with will
He aspired to climb tallest hill
His teacher wasn't a book
Nor his school seemed to be bound
He learnt it from every scar and wound
As moving on
Was his only wish.

A wish based on his belief
Subsiding his life with all the grief
He set a tone to his life
And turned out to be his own chief.

-Born Maverick

OH GIRL.

Oh girl, not a drop of tear
You ain't meant to cry, oh dear
Your struggle is the virtue of sheer
Let go that specter of fear.
A step over step,
You will fare it well
Give yourself the same love
You spent over others to excel.
Never you be hurt
Never you fail

You are an achiever
Show your mettle to all.
Pain is never ending
And so is your grit
Your smiles are precious
Which make the world lit.

-Born Maverick

FORTITUDE

A profuse dust of timely wound
Settling over her tender soul
As her outlook turned vulnerable
Under the shadows of reliance
But she stopped, paused and marched
With all the zeal of building realm
As she woke up to the new dawn
By shredding all her scars
And unleashing her real fortitude.

Finding strength in her brokenness
Was her newly adapted attitude.

-Born Maverick

UPSURGE

I saw the pain melting
In her profound eyes
As she was destined to love.

Every moment was her rise
As she found a reason in every fall
A heart stitched with all wounds
She laced it with her own aura
As her heart still searched for love
Not to retreat at dusk
But to upsurge at the brink of dawn.

This time,
Her heart wanted an assurance
To stay forever.

-Born Maverick

I BREATHE AGAIN

In you,
I found a reason to live
A reason to write
As every word I scribbled
Was my breath for life
And your muse formed my heart.

Every time I decided not to write
I suffocated to reality
Only to find my heart
Filter every emotion out
And rushing it back to veins.
Here I write again,
And hence
I breathe again.

-Born Maverick

J.A. Lyon

J.A. Lyon is a mother of two beautiful children who lives in Long Beach, California. Originally from Oklahoma, she has fallen in love with her new home and feels beyond blessed to live amongst such beauty. Writing has always helped her sort out the chaos swirling in her head, but poetry found her in the dark depths of her heart. She feels indebted to the many brilliant and brave souls who embraced her in her brokenness, and aspires to repay this debt through her own words and help others find hope in a time when they may be struggling to cope.

STOIC SENTINEL

noble sparrow at my window
tell me what you've seen
unlock this cage of ignorance
tell me i am free

like a stoic sentinel
standing guard
you silently watch over me,
waiting patiently

weary though you must be
you carry on your duty
i'm listening
but you don't sing
instead you spread your wings

how many secrets do you keep
voyeuring all
of my harrowing despair
yet telling no one that i'm scared

-J.A. Lyon

ADHERE TO THE WALL

the humming, huddled voices
of the collective string of lies
returns each time i wake
and lift my heavy eyes
but i resist the urge
to hide and find a thimble
of courage inside to climb
the wall of mumbled sighs
become like ivy spreading
growing up and out
across the grumbling garden
wall of stone and grout
its gritty, mortared seams and
hope-soaked dreams with which
i weave my intricate web of mortal screams
i stitch these insecurities
into my mind with laced-up thoughts
and romanticized eulogies

-J.A. Lyon

A FLOWER IN THE DESERT

edges worn
tattered and torn
standing strong through a rainless storm
wanting to cry
she smiles instead
striving for purpose
she raises her head

the day is long,
dreary and bleak
she dare not speak as her patience has peaked
too many days begin like this
not enough nights end with a kiss

a flower growing in the desert
seeking sustenance in a barren land
searching for water among dry sand

she assimilates to this harsh, hot place
requiring less and still showing grace
waiting on the rain to come
she clings to the hope
of drinking some
a trickle,
a drop,
or maybe a few
she doesn't need much,
but it's well overdue

her petals are wilting
the leaves drying up
yet still she survives
with an empty cup

-J.A. Lyon

VAGABOND LOVE

he wanders this town
gathering pieces of others'
unwanted emotions
digging through rubbish
scanning the gutters
a Frankenstein of feelings
stitched together with people's
discarded passions
wadded up napkins
crumbs of good intentions
scattered and scavenged
for the monster he's creating
ready to ravage and romance
any unsuspecting bystander
with his secondhand sorrys
and repurposed remnants
of a love he could never recreate

-J.A. Lyon

ENTANGLED

Upon this dreary bed of thorns I lie
Entangled in the barren, fruitless vines
Hollow voices echo through the chamber
Shut heavy doors of olive wood and twine

-J.A. Lyon

SPROUTING WEEDS

dirt under fingernails
polished and pink
raking through cold, dark
earth while she sings
tugging at weeds
plucking them out
she toils in vain
as they continue to sprout
from each part of the garden
each place that she's touched
her tender excavations
are still too much
she brushes back soil
searching for roots
anything really that resembles the truth
trusses of long white curls, hanging low
touching her pearls
they continue to grow
falling down her cheek with the tears
that water the sprouting weeds
as they have for many years

-J.A. Lyon

EXCAVATED

under the dirt,
entombed and patient,
i wait in vain to be
excavated from the earth
for you to see my worth
brush me off, make me shine
forget that there was once a time
that i was buried deep inside
the hollows of your empty mind

-J.A. Lyon

SACK FULL OF SORRY'S

she carries her demons around
in a sack /of self-destruction/
slung over one shoulder
heavy with doubts, apologies,
and unimaginable losses
shoved in there among all
her broken promises

and the pages
all the pages of words about him

-J.A. Lyon

THE SILENT STRUGGLE

it takes a special kind of
    strength
  to keep going
              forward
        when everything in you
      wants to
pull back
    to fight against the fear
    and to do it with
            grace
    so that not a soul would guess
that inside you are doing
              battle

-J.A. Lyon

OPPOSITES ATTRACT

loyalty will always find its way to the unfaithful
    forgiveness will seek out the unforgiving
        honor will hunt down the wicked
        ambition aims for the apathetic
      truth will track down the deceptive

            and love,
            /i hope/
        love will always find its way
            to the forsaken

            -J.A. Lyon

MATCHSTICK MAN

i ran from a broken man
to one made of matchsticks
jagged ones that leave splinters
and explode on the first strike
but never will i seek to
light a fire with a man again
it can never shine as bright
as the glow that burns within

-J.A. Lyon

SIGNS OF HOPE

and what of the statues
that guard your garden
are they meant to warn me
or do they signal hope
angels toil in cloaked reserve
i've heard they are called
saints of the soil

-J.A. Lyon

RISE

to push, to pursue
rather than shrink and yield
to rise when they
expect you to fall

-J.A. Lyon

HOME

Can you even see the glow?
How I shine
beneath this veil
of raven-feathered lace?
Can you even see my face?

Can you even watch me grow?
Do you have the time,
the patience to embrace me
for as long as I can take it?
Can you tell me I am home?

-J.A. Lyon

SOOTHING

it was the kind of love
that shakes you
out of a deep sleep
to say

"i am here"

the kind that wakes you
from a nightmare
and holds you
through the fear

-J.A. Lyon

DISTRACTED

digging trenches in the field
plowing endless rows
sunshine drenches his whole world
in vibrant shades of gold

.

something small
catches his eye
a simple, yellow butterfly
his calloused hands
and leathery skin
are distracted
from the task again

.

for the man has always been entranced
by all the little things,
and their lovely little dance,
and their pretty little wings

.

his eyes trail along
as the butterfly flies
he smiles
as it crosses the sunrise
slowly now, she passes by
he notices a look in her eye

.

suddenly he feels a twinge,
the pulling of a string
and imagery of them
flashes, flutters on the screen

.

he sees his life with her
in long-lashed smiling eyes,
laughter at the kitchen sink
he grabs playfully at her sides

.

he opens up his eyes again
rays of sun heat up his skin
or is it her
ethereal light,
the chaotic path
of a butterfly's flight

.

digging and plowing
the fields as he goes
back to seeding
these endless rows

.

watching her walk
on down the path
he drops his shovel
and never looks back

.

-J.A. Lyon

MOTHER'S GARDEN

and when she's feeling sad
or lonely
she goes into her garden
and thanks the flowers
for blooming

how lovely
to thank something
for just existing

-J.A. Lyon

GROW UP

look to the light as the stems
and the flowers do
face the warm sun and grow up

-J.A. Lyon

REBIRTH

she sees strength and beauty
in the knowledge
that is annually confirmed

that though the petals fall
and the leaves wither
they will bloom again
when the winter thaws

it is a cycle
and never are we finished
growing
we break, but become stronger
our regrowth thicker
producing more buds and
multiplying our beauty

hope eternally blooms
providing us a chance to
begin again

-J.A. Lyon

B.E. Sampson

Brandon E. Sampson was born and raised in the Coachella Valley of Southern California, which is home to the world's largest music festival known as The Coachella Fest.

Growing up in a home where both his parents were musicians, Brandon found a love for writing, producing, and performing music, as well as poetry, and prose.

He says, "since I was a kid, I've needed some sort of creative outlet to maintain my sanity, and writing has always been the bridge between my subconscious and conscious thought; it's the seeing of sounds yet to be tasted; the profound within the profanity. Writing has been a lot of things to me, but it has never been just a compilation of words. It's healing, it's connection, it's revealing, and has become the articulation of my heart and minds struggle to often process and reconcile with the diverse seasons life can bring. Writing is my voice when I can't speak."

A LETTER TO MEND

In hopes you can feel me,
I pour my heart out in Braille.
Yet in fear of rejection,
I hide the truth between these lines.
And while my everything yearns to be yours,
I pray you read this
with your eyes closed and heart open.
I pray you feel my soul
in every line I've hidden between.
And when you come to the end of this letter,
I hope you will know me a little truer,
a little deeper, between the insecurities
that've long clouded my words
with the many fears of even sharing them with you. Please hear me
and not the letters I've written to send.
Please hear the longing in my silence
that screams to heal.

-B.E.Sampson

THE COMPOSITION OF EMPATHY

You are not broken or overly sensitive.
You are the perfect composition
of compassion and empathy,
and without you, hearts would heal a lot slower.
It's the sensitivity and depth of love you hold in your heart, and on
the tip of your tongue,
that knowingly or not,
moves brokenness back together
every time you simply breathe.

-B.E.Sampson

THE SOUND OF TRUTH

I choose not swords but words,

and kill them with kindness.
With thought provoking sounds
I'll explode their minds,
and unbind their fists with truth.

-B.E.Sampson

IF ONLY FOR ONE

I've always hoped that my heart would be heard by another, and
for my words to bring healing and understanding to a soul. It is not
for the masses that I write, or share my heart, but for the one
broken soul that is longing for a chance to find wholeness again. I
want that connection to be real. And if for only one, I would share
my whole heart, with words, or in silence.

-B.E.Sampson

SHE IS EVERYTHING THEY WISH THEY COULD BE

She is everything they wish they could be

She believes in the impossible

And makes the unattainable tangible

Because she refuses to limit her potential

To only what they believe is attainable

To merely a system of beliefs

For they are stuck

in what they perceive cannot be

Because their system forbids them

To believe in anything they are not told to believe in

She is what she believes she can be

So she is everything

And that

They only wish they could be

-B.E.Sampson

WRAPPED AROUND ME

I need more than your eloquent words
to calm the palpitations in my chest.
I need your heartbeat wrapped around me,
and your gentle smile to penetrate my insecurities.

-B.E.Sampson

DELIVERANCE

Unfold me

Find my creases

Move your lips across my bent and broken

Envelope my closed until there is nothing left but open

Lay me down upon your words of hope and healing

And let your presence become the soothe to my breathing

-B.E.Sampson

THE HAND OF EXPERIENCE

We don't deserve anything
we aren't willing to give first.
Because if we've never held the hand
of experience, our stories won't be worth
a second glance.

-B.E.Sampson

TAKE IT OFF

Take off all of your clothes,

and all of the makeup you use

to cover all of the fears you've been told to never let show.

Expose your soul.

Lay bare everything that our culture tells you

will make you undesirable.

It's not what you wear that makes me want you,

but it's the heart you expose that makes me love you.

-B.E.Sampson

VALUE OF THORNS

Life is like a bed of roses, beautiful.
Sometimes it feels and smells so lovely, and sometimes it's
a bloody back full of thorns.
But either way there is beauty,
you just have to value the thorns.

-B.E.Sampson

ME

I smile with my eyes,
and my heart speaks through them.
I love beyond words,
yet I move souls with them.
I'm a silent smile,
but a heart full.

-B.E.Sampson

LIFE IS A METAPHOR

I don't have time for bitterness.

Anger and hate, they limit my dreams from becoming the salvation
my heart needs to breathe.
I don't have time for resentment, for it only keeps me bound to
what has happened and not what is possible.
Life is too short to hold on to anything that was, for life is the
breath of what is and what will be.

-B.E.Sampson

A SYMPHONY WITHIN

And I'll dance when negative words try to beat me down, for my
rhythm comes not from the sounds around me, but the symphony
within me.

-B.E.Sampson

THE SPIRIT OF REDEMPTION

Within the darkest of depths
We must sow seeds of forgiveness
Letting life itself crack apart
All the pieces and shadows
That hide our healing
From the arms of the spirit
Who continually pours redemption
Upon the roots of all creation

-B.E.Sampson

DARE TO DREAM

He once sat on the council of Lords and Kings
Until his dreams defined a direction beyond what their conjured
control could contain
So to exile he was maimed
For believing
For seeing past the authority they self proclaimed
And as he was banished from sitting at their table
Rumors and stories began to unfade
Like a dirty mirror distorting the truth of ones shape
Yet once it's touched with the cloth of clarity
The detail of its royal reflection is brought to reign
And so one by one the common folk snuck away
From the oppressive disarray of the Lords and Kings
To follow a heart that so dared to dream
That dared to believe in anything but the mundane

-B.E.Sampson

YOUR WORDS

Your words may not have been written from the steps your feet
have taken,
but your words guide and comfort the paths of many who know
not even how to articulate their pain and struggles.
Your words are a beacon of light,
and they shine from the beauty
and devastation your soul has been through.
So even though your words don't always parallel your path, they
compose healing and direction for the daunting journey others may
be facing.

-B.E.Sampson

JUST WRITE

When you write your heart out, however broken or whole, you're
planting seeds in more places than you could possibly know you've
sown. Some will die, some grow, but first you have to be willing
to pour your heart out with no possible resolve upon the horizon.
Too many times we keep our hearts in cages; if broken, we hide
behind depression and shame; if whole, we withhold in fear of ever
being broken again.
Write it out, whatever it may be.
Let your words plant seeds in others, and in your own heart, but
first you have to let go of all expectations
but one...
Just write.

-B.E.Sampson

LOVE LET ME BE ME

Love let me fly;
it gave me reason to die.
Love shed truth on lies that kept my heart hidden;
It lit my soul with passion beyond perception.
Love connected the dots
when all rhyme and reason
had been fractionalized
by the lines of reality.
But love colored beyond the lines,
exposing beauty outside of them,
for it saw in and between the limits
I defined as worthy of being loved.
Love accepted me for who I am,
not who I was or could be,
but love let me be, me.

-B.E.Sampson

-*Author Information*-

To stay up to date with your favorite writers from this anthology, please check them out on their various writing forums listed below.

Kevin Vargo
- Instagram   @kevinvargo_

CD
- Instagram   @poemandpeonies

K, Waters
- Instagram   @itskabes

-Hooves-
- Instagram   @poetwithbooves
- Facebook   Poetwithhooves

Kimmery Moss
- Instagram   @kimmerywrites
- Blog   kimmerymoss.com

Alice Foster
- Instagram   @nebulahymns
- Blog   www. pseudosaint. tumblr. com

J.B.
- Instagram   @jeremybrown21
                   @wordsfromgeorgia

Born Maverick
- Instagram   @bornmaverick
- Blog   www.theprose.com/Born_maverick
- Twitter   azhar_murtuza

J.A. Lyon
- Instagram   @j_a_lyon
                @jenn_speed85

B.E. Sampson
- Instagram   @my_paper_trails
- Email   Info.MyPaperTrails@gmail.com